Editorial planning
Jollands Editions

SCHOOLHOUSE PRESS, Inc.

Designed and produced by BLA Publishing Limited,
Swan Court, East Grinstead, Sussex, England.
Also in LONDON · HONG KONG · TAIPEI · SINGAPORE · NEW YORK
A Ling Kee Company

Illustrations by Kevin Diaper, Jack Pelling/Linden Artists,
  Chris Rothero/Linden Artists, David Thompson/Linden Artists,
  Brian Watson/Linden Artists and BLA Publishing Limited
Color origination by Chris Willcock Reproductions
Printed and bound in Spain by
Gráficas Estella, S. A. Navarra.
                                          6 5 4 3 2 1

86/87/88/89

Acknowledgements
**The Publishers wish to thank the following
organizations for their invaluable assistance in the
preparation of this book.**

Australian Information Service, London
Canadian High Commission

Photographic credits
t = top b = bottom l = left r = right

cover: ZEFA

4 Ed Lawrenson; 5 ZEFA; 8 The Hutchison Library; 9,
10 ZEFA; 11 South American Pictures; 12*t* The
Hutchison Library; 12*b*, 13 ZEFA; 16 John Lythgoe/
Seaphot; 17 Jonathan Scott/Seaphot; 18 Australian
Information Service; 19, 20, 21 ZEFA; 22 The Hutchison
Library; 23 David George/ Seaphot; 26 The Hutchison
Library; 27*t* Douglas Dickens; 27*b* ZEFA; 28 Douglas
Dickens; 29*t*, 29*b* The Hutchison Library; 30 ZEFA; 31
Douglas Dickens; 32*t*, 32*b*, 33 ZEFA; 34 ANT/NHPA;
34/35 Australian Information Service; 36*t*, 36*b*, 37 South
American Pictures; 39*t* Alex Williams/Seaphot; 39*b* ZEFA;
41*t* Canadian High Commission; 41*b* Douglas Dickens;
42, 43 The Hutchison Library; 44 ZEFA; 45 David
George/Seaphot

Note to the reader
In this book there are some words in the text which are printed in **bold** type. This shows that the
word is listed in the glossary on page 46. The glossary gives a brief explanation of words which may
be new to you.

Contents

Introduction

Water is all around us. It is in the oceans, seas, rivers, and lakes. There is water deep under the ground. Water is in the clouds above us. Huge amounts of water are frozen in the **ice caps** of the North and South Poles. If water covers three quarters of the earth, why is there sometimes a shortage?

Most of the earth's water is in the seas and oceans. The problem is that seawater contains salt. You can use salt to cook with, but if you drink a glass of salt water, it will make you sick. The salt has to be taken out before you can drink it. Many countries cannot afford to make drinking water from salt water.

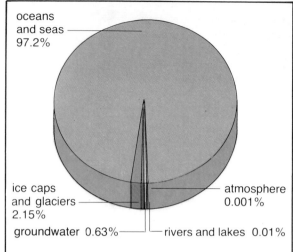

oceans and seas 97.2%

ice caps and glaciers 2.15%

atmosphere 0.001%

groundwater 0.63%

rivers and lakes 0.01%

You can see from this chart that most of the earth's water is salty. We can use only a small amount of the fresh water. The rest is either under the ground or frozen in the ice caps.

▼ **Antarctica is about one and a half times bigger than the United States. Most of the land is covered by ice which is 6,500 feet thick.**

► This land in Egypt would look like the desert beyond, without the Nile River. All the trees you can see get their water from the river.

Fresh Water

The water people and animals need for drinking is called **fresh water**. Crops also need fresh water. Less than 3 per cent of the world's water is fresh. Most of the earth's fresh water is frozen in ice caps and **glaciers**. Glaciers are rivers of solid ice.

So where does the water we use come from? Some of it comes from the rivers and the lakes. Look at pages 24 and 25 and you will see where some of the longest rivers and largest lakes are in the world. Some of the water comes from under the ground. This is called **groundwater**. We get this water from wells. The fresh water in the clouds falls as rain or snow. It replaces some of the water we get from under the ground.

Different Uses of Water

Water is important in many ways. People need to drink water to live. Anyone lost in the desert without water would die in a few days. Water is used for washing and cooking and for heating our homes. Plants could not grow without water. Farmers have to water, or **irrigate**, their crops if there is not enough rain.

Industry needs a large amount of fresh water. Food, drinks, paper, and clothes are made using water. Many factory machines have to be cooled by water. The machines which make **electricity** in power plants are driven by strong jets of **steam**. The steam is produced by heating water.

Sometimes **chemicals** and other wastes are pumped into the rivers. The water becomes dirty. Then, a valuable supply of fresh water is spoiled. The wastes also kill the plants and fish. Many countries have stopped factories from pouring wastes into the rivers. Even so, it will take time for the rivers to become clean again.

The Water Cycle

Water is always moving. It moves across the ground, in the air, and in the sea. This movement is called the **water cycle**. This is the way the seas, rivers, and lakes are filled up again by rain and snow.

The water in streams and rivers flows downhill to the sea. Groundwater flows downhill, too. Why does it do this? If you throw a ball up into the air, the earth's **gravity** pulls it back to the ground. Gravity also pulls water from the high ground down to the sea.

Rain and Snow

Water must change to get into the air. Before it can change, it needs heat. When you boil water in a kettle, the water changes into steam, or **evaporates**. The same thing happens when the sun shines on the seas, rivers, and lakes. The sun's

snow

rain

groundwater

heat makes some of the water turn to steam, or water **vapor**. The warm vapor rises up into the air until it meets cold air. The cold air cools the vapor. Look at the steam from a boiling kettle. What happens if the steam hits a cold window? It changes back into water, or **condenses**. The drops of water on the window make **condensation**.

When the warm vapor rising from the earth hits the cold air, it condenses into a lot of tiny drops. The drops make clouds. If the clouds rise higher, the drops within them grow bigger. These heavy drops of water fall back to the ground as rain. Sometimes, the clouds rise even higher. The air is so cold that the drops turn to ice. They fall back to the ground as snow.

The rain and melting snow fill up the seas, rivers, and lakes. The sun's heat makes the water evaporate again.

Where Rain Falls

Rain does not fall evenly across the world. Most rain falls on land near the coast. This is because most water vapor comes from the sea. Winds blow the clouds towards the warm land. The heat from the land makes the clouds rise and turn into rain. If the clouds are blown towards a mountain, they are pushed higher. This makes the clouds drop their water as rain. The wind blows the clouds over the mountain, but the water has been lost. It hardly rains at all on the other side.

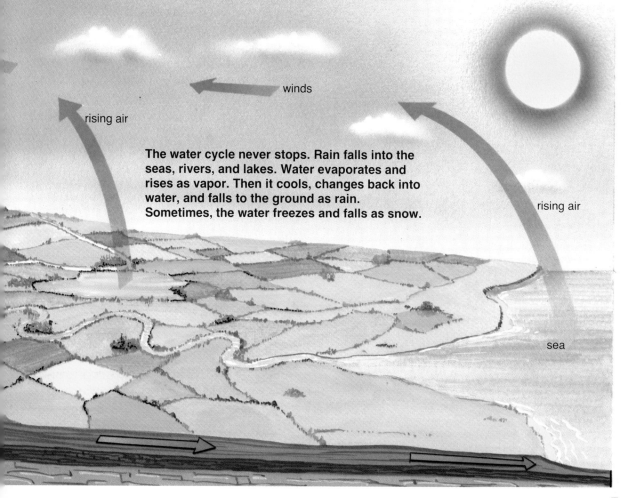

winds

rising air

rising air

The water cycle never stops. Rain falls into the seas, rivers, and lakes. Water evaporates and rises as vapor. Then it cools, changes back into water, and falls to the ground as rain. Sometimes, the water freezes and falls as snow.

sea

The Steep River

Imagine that you are following a river from the high ground to the sea below. The river can be split into three stages, or **reaches**. The river is different at each stage. In the upper reach, the river is born and soon moves very fast. In the middle reach, the river gets wider and slows down. In the lower reach, the river gets even slower. Finally it flows into the sea.

The River Begins

The start of a river is called the **source**. A river can begin in several places. Many rivers start on high ground, often in the mountains. Their water comes from melting snow and glaciers.

Other rivers begin as **springs**. A spring is a place where water stored under the ground comes to the surface. When rain falls on high ground, it soaks into the earth. Then, it meets layers of rock. Some types of rocks soak up the water. Others do not. The water sinks as far as it can. Then, it flows sideways. At last, it reaches the side of the hill or mountain and trickles out as a spring.

The young river is joined by many small streams called **tributaries**. The river gets wider as more streams flow into it. The river flows very fast in the upper reach. It rushes straight down the mountain. The water carries loose stones along. The rushing water and the stones cut a channel through the rocky ground. The channel deepens slowly. The river cuts a **valley** with steep sides in the shape of a V. This wearing away of the land is called **erosion**.

Waterfalls

When the river comes to a steep drop, it tumbles over the edge in a shower of water. This is called a waterfall. Waterfalls are often formed when a river flows first over a layer of hard rock and then over a layer of soft rock. The water wears away the soft rock first. The hard rock left on top makes

▲ This V-shaped valley has been carved by the young river. The rushing water washes loose stones down the river. Most of the river's water comes from the mountains in the distance.

a ledge. The water tumbles over the ledge. From time to time, pieces of the ledge fall away. In this way, the waterfall slowly moves back up the river.

Waterfalls also appear where there is a weak point in the land which makes it crack. These cracks are called **faults**. One part of the land is pushed up higher than the other. It makes a cliff.

Rapids

As the river flows on, it sometimes gets stirred up as it passes through rocky areas called **rapids**. Rapids are made where there is a mixture of hard and soft rocks together on the river bed. The water wears away the soft rocks. The hard rocks are left jutting out like pointed steps, and the water rushes over them.

▼ The famous Niagara Falls in North America are 195 feet high. 10,000 years ago, they tumbled into Lake Ontario. Now, they have moved about seven miles up the river.

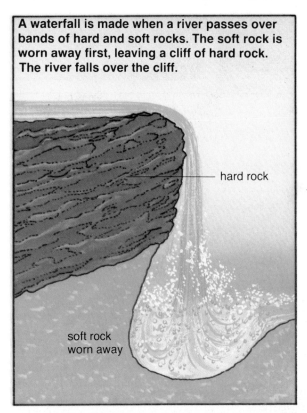

A waterfall is made when a river passes over bands of hard and soft rocks. The soft rock is worn away first, leaving a cliff of hard rock. The river falls over the cliff.

hard rock

soft rock worn away

The River Valley

▼ The Mosel River in Germany joins the Rhine River at Koblenz. Here, a bridge links two small towns on either side of the river. The sides of the valley in the background are too steep for houses to be built on them.

On your journey down the river you will notice that the river changes when it gets to the middle reach. In the river valley, the ground is less steep so the river slows down. The water is calm. The river gets wider. The land near the river is good for farming. Although the hillsides are sometimes too steep to build houses on, people have settled near the water. There are towns and villages along the banks. People use the river to travel on. Ships and boats of all kinds sail up and down. The river is full of life.

The Valley Widens

In the upper reach, the young river cuts straight down the mountain. Now the river winds its way through the hills. It still cuts a path downhill. At the same time the river gets wider. The tributaries empty more water, soil, and stones into the river. As the water, soil, and stones flow past the river banks they begin to cut away, or erode, them. Rivers erode the land very slowly. The Colorado River has taken nearly 10 million years to cut out the Grand Canyon in Arizona.

outside bank
worn away

soil
and
stones

inside bank

A Change of Course

The river now begins to swing from side to side, or **meander**. At first, the river swings in gentle loops. The water on the inside of the bend flows slowly. This slowly moving water drops, or **deposits**, soil and stones along the banks. The water on the outside flows quickly. It has more cutting power. This means that the outside bend will erode faster. Over the years, the course of the river slowly changes. The river erodes more and more of the bend until it cuts straight through to the other side of the loop.

◄ The bends in a river become greater as the water erodes the outside banks and drops soil on the inside. This makes the river slowly change its course.

▼ The river bank is being steadily worn away by erosion. The earth was cut away from under the fallen tree.

The Flat Lands

The river is old now. The end of its journey is near. In the lower reach, it winds slowly through a wide, flat valley to the sea. This valley is called a **flood plain**. The river is very wide. It still carries very fine pieces of stone and soil along with it, but they have been ground up by the water into a mixture of fine sand and mud. This is called **silt**. The river flows too slowly for the silt to erode the banks.

The Flood Plain

After heavy rains, the river water rises and spills over the banks. It floods the plain. A layer of silt is dropped all over the land. As water pours over the banks on to the plain, a lot of harm is done. Sometimes, people lose their homes and their crops.

The flooding of the plains can also help the people who live there. The silt that comes from the river is very **fertile**. This means that it is full of things which make plants grow. Farmers can grow crops like cotton, sugar cane, and rice on the fertile flood plain.

The river also drops piles of silt on the banks when it floods. The banks become

▲ Heavy monsoon rains fall in Burma from June to September. The heavy rains make the Irrawaddy River flood. Large areas of farmland are covered with water.

◀ A muddy river meanders slowly across a flood plain in Brazil. You can see the river in the distance has almost looped back on itself. Crops are growing on the fertile land.

▶ Lots of channels and small islands make up a river delta. The building gives an idea of the size of the delta.

higher each year. Layers of silt build up on the river bed. In this way, the level of the river slowly rises. After a time, the river flows in a channel above the level of the flood plain. This has happened to the Mississippi River and to the Hwang Ho in China.

The River Mouth

The part of the river that enters the sea is called the river mouth. Some rivers have wide mouths called **estuaries**. The level of the river changes with the **tides**. At high tide, the sea rushes up the estuary to meet the river flowing towards it. At low tide, the sea draws back, and the river bed can be seen.

The river slows down as it enters the sea. It drops more silt. The sea washes most of the silt away. The silt found in estuaries can make marshy **mudflats**. The silt can also cut off areas of water, making lakes called **lagoons**.

Some rivers, such as the Nile and the Mississippi, drop so much silt that the sea cannot wash it away. Piles of silt build up on the seabed and form new land. The river mouth becomes a marshy plain. The river fans out into small channels which force their way through the silt. This region of channels is called a **delta**. The name for this type of river mouth comes from the shape of the fourth letter of the Greek alphabet, delta Δ.

Life in a River

Rivers are full of wildlife. Many types of animals live in the water and on the banks. In the upper reach, the river flows very fast. Only a few plants and animals can live in the rushing water. The trout is a strong fish. It can swim against the flow of the river. The young, or **larvae**, of insects cling to the rocks.

In the middle reach, the water slows down. It is calmer. Plants are able to put roots down into the river bed. The plants give food and shelter for fish. More groups, or **shoals**, of fish are found.

In the lower reach, the water flows very slowly. In some rivers, flowers like water lilies float on the still water. Water birds can swim easily. The birds nest in the rushes that grow by the water's edge. Water **mammals**, like otters, live on the river banks.

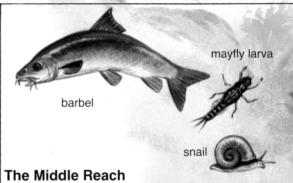

barbel

mayfly larva

snail

The Middle Reach

More plants and water weeds can take root in the calmer waters of the middle reach. The fish are strong swimmers. The barbel likes clear rivers where the bed is sand or gravel. It lives near the bottom of the river and feeds on mayfly larvae, snails, and water plants. Barbels collect in shoals and hide under weeds on the river bed.

The Lower Reach

In the lower reach, long-legged herons wade into the shallow water and wait for fish. They stab the fish with their sharp bills and swallow them whole. Ducks swim around on the still river. There is a blue flash as a kingfisher dives from a tree and catches a fish. Dragonflies hover above the water.

In the water, perch feed on weeds and smaller fish. There are shellfish, like clams and freshwater shrimps. Turtles can be found in the lower reaches of some rivers. A turtle is a **reptile**. It has a thick shell and strong flipper-like legs. It can live in the water, but it lays its eggs on land.

water lilies

14

The Upper Reach

In the upper reach of a river, weeds called **algae** cling to the rocks. Trout swim through the clear water and feed on the larvae of insects, such as the stonefly. A trout swims with a powerful sideways movement of its tail. The dipper nests on the river bank, under a bridge, or behind a waterfall. It perches on a stone in the river and searches for food. When it sees insects or larvae, it dives into the water to catch them. The dipper does not have **webbed feet** like a duck. It can swim on the surface or underwater. The dipper can also walk along the bed of a stream to look for food.

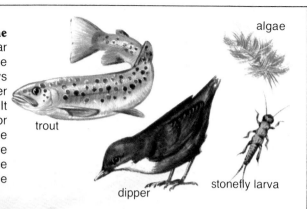

trout

algae

dipper

stonefly larva

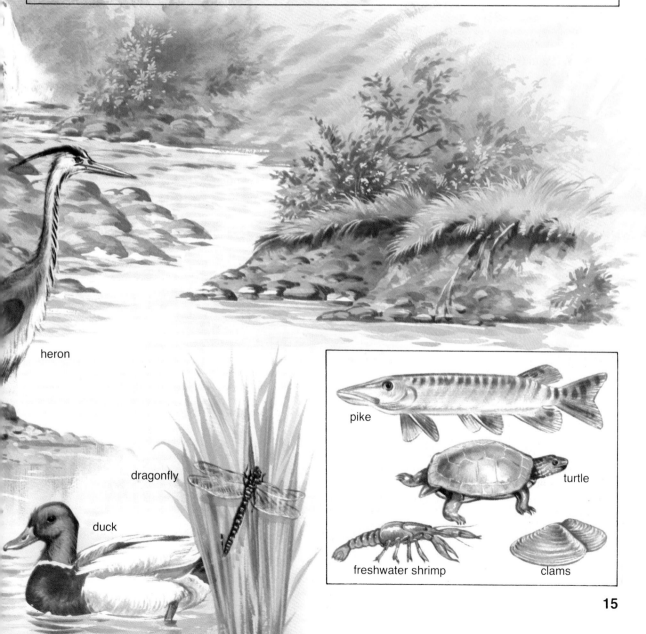

heron

dragonfly

duck

pike

turtle

freshwater shrimp

clams

Life in a Tropical River

Some rivers flow through **tropical** countries where the weather is hot all the year round. The lower reaches of a tropical river are full of fish and plants. There are fierce **predators** on the lookout for food. A predator hunts for other animals to eat. These animals are its **prey**.

Some tropical fish, such as torpedo rays and electric catfish, kill their prey with **electric shocks**. There are also electric eels which can grow to 27 feet long. Frogs and toads live on the river banks. Some of them look just like dead leaves. This keeps them from being eaten by other animals.

River Hunters

Some of the fiercest predators are the crocodiles and alligators. They are reptiles with long bodies and huge snapping jaws. The young feed on fish, but the adults eat any animals.

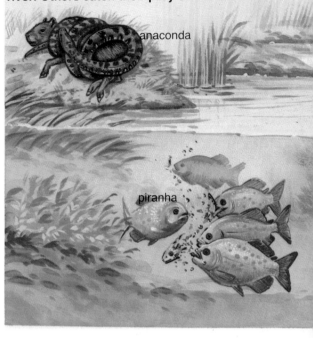

▼ Many predators wait in the water of a tropical river. Others catch their prey on the banks.

anaconda

piranha

Another reptile, the anaconda snake, spends most of its time in the water. It kills animals and birds that come to drink in the river. The snake wraps itself around its prey and stops it from breathing. The

◄ Alligators like to rest in muddy swamps when they are not in the water. Although they are slow on land, they move quickly through the water with the help of their long, powerful tails.

darter

electric catfish

matamata turtle

electric eel

The darter, or anhinga, is a bird with a long thin neck. It feeds on fish. The giant Brazilian otter also catches fish. It has webbed feet and is nearly six feet long.

The South American piranha fish has strong sharp teeth. It will attack any animal that is swimming in the river.

The Hippopotamus

The hippopotamus lives in Africa and is the largest freshwater animal. Hippos have large bodies with short legs. They spend their days in the river. Hippos can swim well. They can hold their breath under water for a long time. They float in the water with most of their bodies below the surface. All that can be seen above the water is the top parts of their flat heads. At night, they move slowly along the banks in search of food. They eat grass and other plants.

South American matamata turtle hides in the muddy water and looks like a lump of dead wood. If a fish comes near, the turtle opens its mouth wide and snaps up the fish.

▼ These hippos may look quite small, but hippos can weigh as much as 8,800 pounds. This is more than the weight of 60 people.

Rivers in Flood

Most floods are caused by heavy rain. Rivers get so full that they burst their banks. In some parts of the world, there is very heavy rain once or twice a year and no rain at all for the rest of the time. The ground gets very hard and dry. When the rains come, the water cannot soak into the hard ground. This causes sudden **flash floods**. The floods do a lot of harm because no one is ready for them.

Flood Control

Floods often can be held back. A **dam** can be built higher up a river. A dam is a strong wall which holds the river back. The water behind the dam forms a lake called a **reservoir**. The water is stored in the reservoir until it is needed. If there is a dry period, the river level goes down. Passages, called **sluice gates**, in the wall of the dam are opened. Then, the water in the lake flows into the river.

Some rivers flood at the same places each year. The high banks, or **levees**, of these rivers are built up so that they are higher than the flood level. This is the level that the flood water has reached in the past. Barriers, called **floodgates**, are sometimes built across a river estuary. The floodgates hold back the sea at high tide and stop the water from flooding the land.

▼ Alice Springs, in Australia, is a dry place for most of the year. Sudden heavy rains have made the Todd River burst its banks.

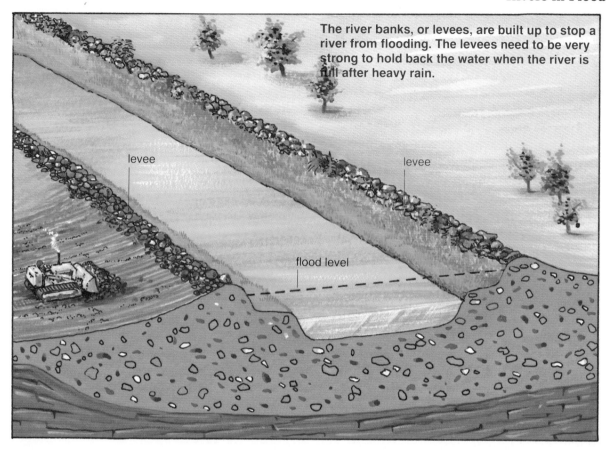

The river banks, or levees, are built up to stop a river from flooding. The levees need to be very strong to hold back the water when the river is full after heavy rain.

levee

levee

flood level

Draining the Land

When the river floods the plain, the water often takes a long time to go away. Some land becomes a wet, marshy **swamp** which never dries out. The swampy land has to be **drained** before it can be used. Ditches, called **dikes**, are dug to carry the water away from the land. In the Netherlands, windmills once pumped the water from the land into waterways called **canals**. Today, machines pump the water.

People use the drained land for farming. Houses are built, and soon the flood plain looks very different. Even so, the risk of flooding never goes away completely.

◀ Row upon row of ditches drain this land so that it can be used for farming. The building you can see has been built on a low hill to protect it from floods.

River Power

Have you ever swum in a river? You may remember how the flow of the river tried to force you along with it. River flow, or power, has been used by people for thousands of years. Long ago, people sat on floating logs to carry them down a river. Today, the cheapest way to get trees to a sawmill is to float them down a river.

Waterwheels

River power has been used to turn waterwheels for centuries. There are two types of waterwheels. One type is the **undershot** wheel. The lower part of the wheel rests in the river. The flow of the water pushes the wheel around.

The other type is the **overshot** wheel. It does not rest in the river. The water has to come from above. This type of wheel needs to be built where the river is steep. There are buckets attached to the outside of the wheel. The water from the river flows along a chute which ends above the wheel.

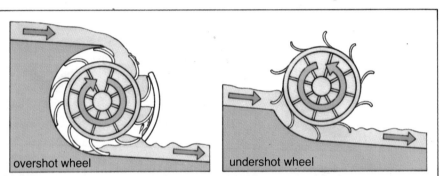

overshot wheel

undershot wheel

◀ An undershot wheel turns slowly with the flow of the river. The overshot wheel works better because the water drops into the buckets from above. The falling water makes the wheel turn faster.

▶ These undershot waterwheels are being used for irrigation in Portugal. The wheels are turned by the flow of the river. The water is scooped up in the buckets as the wheels turn.

The water falls from the chute and drops into one of the buckets. The bucket fills up and its weight pulls it down. Another bucket takes its place, and so on. The weight of the full buckets turns the wheel.

Electricity from Water

The modern type of waterwheel is the water **turbine**. A turbine is a wheel with blades. Water turbines are used to drive machines which make electricity. It is made at a **hydroelectric** power plant using the power of the water.

A turbine needs a fast flow of water to drive the machines. A dam is built across the river at a place where the water is rushing downhill. The water forms a lake behind the dam. When the sluice gates of the dam open, the water rushes into the turbine, strikes the blades, and makes the turbine turn.

▶ The Hoover Dam is built across the Colorado River in Nevada. It is 718 feet high and 3,978 feet long. The dam supplies water for hydroelectricity, irrigation, and homes. The dam also controls flooding.

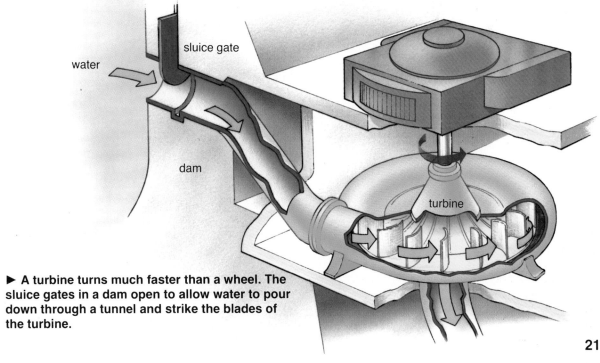

▶ A turbine turns much faster than a wheel. The sluice gates in a dam open to allow water to pour down through a tunnel and strike the blades of the turbine.

People and Rivers

The world's longest rivers may pass through more than one country. These rivers are important to the people who live and work along their banks. Some of the rivers are wide enough for large **cargo** ships to use them. Towns and cities have been built where ships load and unload their goods. The Amazon River in Brazil flows through thick jungle. People living farther up the river travel by water because there are few roads.

Wide rivers are difficult to cross, so they can protect people living along their banks from attack. When a river is used as a border, there may be border posts on each side of the bridge crossing the river.

Opening Up the Rivers

When early explorers found new lands, they sailed along the coast until they came to a river. They used the rivers as "roads" inland. Some of them settled near the rivers. The river and the fertile land nearby gave them all they needed to live.

It is not easy to steer, or **navigate**, a ship along a river. There are banks of mud or sand where ships can run aground. People called river **pilots** steer the ships up the river. The pilot knows about the tides and where the river is shallow. The pilot can guide the ship along the safe, deep channels.

Some rivers become clogged with silt. Machines called **dredgers** are used to remove the silt. The dredgers keep the deep channel open for the bigger ships.

▼ Two barges full of goods make their way up the Yangtze-Kiang River in China. It is easier to transport heavy goods by river than by road in hilly country.

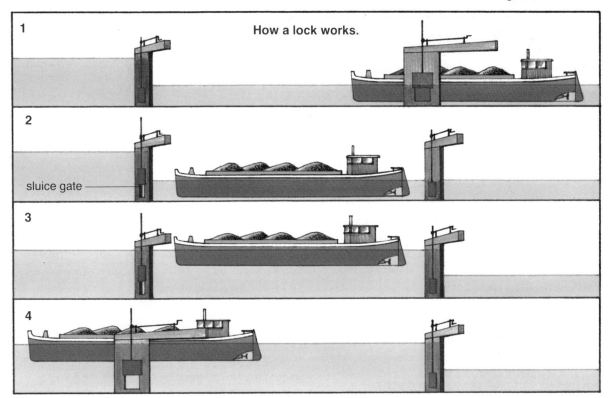

How a lock works.

1. Barge enters lock at lower level.
2. Lock gates closed and sluice gates opened.
3. Barge rises to higher level.
4. Lock gates open, barge leaves at higher level.

▼ The 211-foot iron bridge at Ironbridge, England. It was designed by Abraham Darby. He was the first person to use iron to make a bridge.

Locks have to be built where the river is steep. A lock is like a step. The ship enters the lock. Gates close behind it. Water is let in, or let out, to lift the ship up or down. The gates are opened, and the ship sails out.

Crossing Rivers

People have always wanted to cross rivers as well as to travel along them. The first bridges were tree trunks laid down across streams.

The world's first iron bridge was built across the Severn River in England in 1779. The town called Ironbridge has grown up by the side of the bridge.

Many towns on rivers have the word "bridge" hidden in their names. Towns, such as Bridgwater, Cambridge, and Stonebridge, grew up where a river could be bridged. If it is not possible to build a bridge, boats called **ferries** carry people and goods across the river.

Rivers, Lakes, and Dams

Rivers and Lakes

The Amazon River is so big that it carries one fifth of the world's fresh water. The Great Lakes of North America form the world's biggest group of lakes. The deepest lake is Lake Baikal in the USSR, which is nearly 6,500 feet in depth. The reservoir which holds the most water is the Bratsk Reservoir in the USSR, but another reservoir in Ghana called Lake Volta covers a wider area. It measures 3,274 square miles.

Waterfalls

Niagara Falls in North America are moving backward 4 feet every year. They

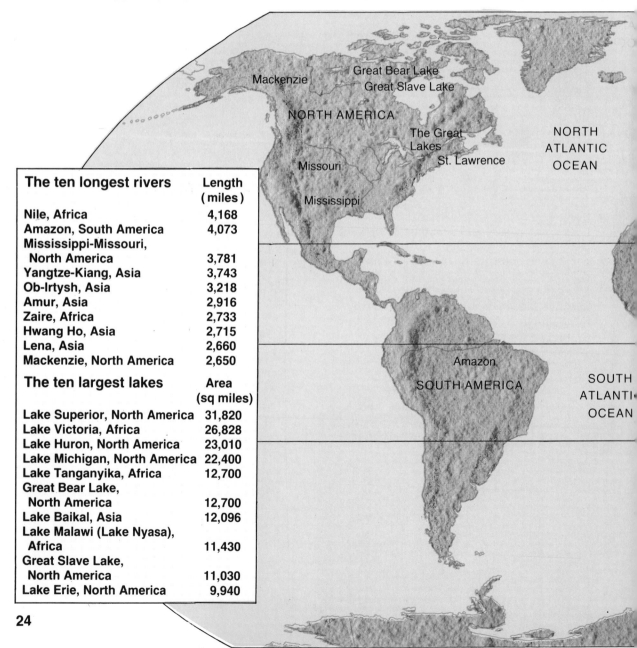

The ten longest rivers	Length (miles)
Nile, Africa	4,168
Amazon, South America	4,073
Mississippi-Missouri, North America	3,781
Yangtze-Kiang, Asia	3,743
Ob-Irtysh, Asia	3,218
Amur, Asia	2,916
Zaire, Africa	2,733
Hwang Ho, Asia	2,715
Lena, Asia	2,660
Mackenzie, North America	2,650

The ten largest lakes	Area (sq miles)
Lake Superior, North America	31,820
Lake Victoria, Africa	26,828
Lake Huron, North America	23,010
Lake Michigan, North America	22,400
Lake Tanganyika, Africa	12,700
Great Bear Lake, North America	12,700
Lake Baikal, Asia	12,096
Lake Malawi (Lake Nyasa), Africa	11,430
Great Slave Lake, North America	11,030
Lake Erie, North America	9,940

have existed for 10,000 years and in that time have moved almost 7 miles upstream. The widest waterfalls are the Khone Falls on the Mekong River in Laos. They are 6¾ miles wide. The spectacular Iguassu Falls in South America are made up of 275 separate waterfalls.

Dams

The world's greatest dam is New Cornelia Tailings Dam in Arizona. It is 97 feet high and 6½ miles long. The largest concrete dam is the Grand Coulee Dam on the Columbia River in the State of Washington. It is 542 feet high and 4,134 feet long. The tallest dam, the Grande Dixence in Switzerland, is 926 feet high. The longest dam is the Yacryeta-Apipe Dam in South America. It is 45 miles long.

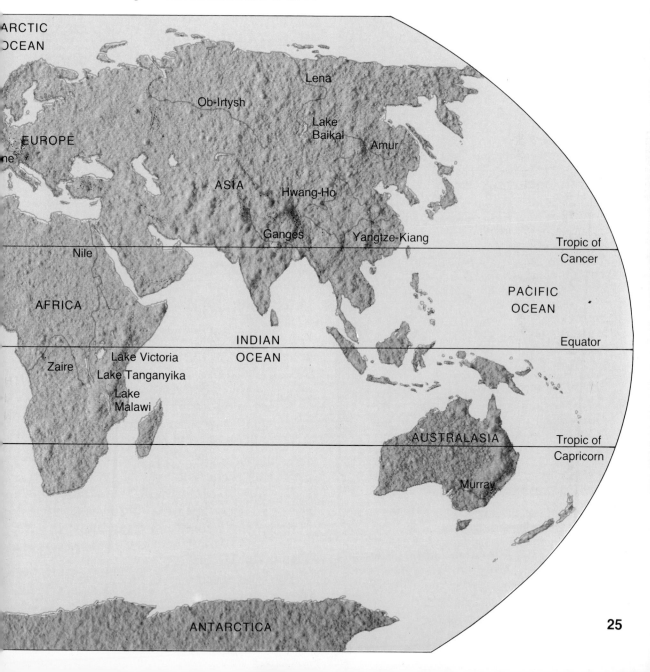

The Nile

The Sahara is the largest desert in the world. It stretches across northern Africa. Egypt lies to the east of the Sahara. Egypt has very little rain. The world's longest river, the Nile, flows through the middle of this dry country.

The Nile begins as two rivers. The White Nile flows from Lake Victoria in Central Africa. The Blue Nile rises in Ethiopia. The rivers meet at Khartoum in the Sudan. The Nile flows through Egypt into the Mediterranean Sea.

Watering the Crops

The "gift of the Nile" was how the Greek historian Herodotus described the Nile in 450 BC. It is Egypt's only river. The Nile gives farmers the water they need for their crops. It also has a fertile delta at its mouth. People have farmed the land beside the Nile for 5,000 years. The river branches into small streams at the delta. The streams divide the land into sections where crops are grown.

The early farmers learned how to use the river. The river flooded every summer between July and November. It dropped rich silt on the land. The people planted seeds in the mud and grew wheat and barley.

A simple way to water the land was invented about 4,000 years ago. It is called the **shaduf**, and it is still used in some places today. The farmer uses a long pole, or **lever**, with weights on the end to lift buckets of water from the river.

The Nile was used as the main way into and out of Egypt. Early ships were made from the **reeds** that grew by the river. Later, the Egyptians built bigger ships out of wood. They then sailed farther and began to **trade** with other Mediterranean lands.

The Nile Today

The river and its delta are still very important for people in Egypt today. Many

▲ The Egyptians have been using some types of irrigation for thousands of years. The shaduf is one type which is still used today. When the rope is pulled, the pole swings down, lowering the bucket into the water. When the rope is let go, the weight at the end of the pole lifts the bucket of water up to ground level.

people are farmers. If you look down on the Nile Valley from a plane, you see two broad green bands on either side of the river. These are where the crops are grown. The desert lies beyond the green bands.

The flooding of the Nile is controlled by the new Aswan High Dam in southern Egypt. The water is stored in Lake Nasser. This huge lake is 313 miles long and stretches into another country, the Sudan. The lake provides water for Egypt and Sudan. The dam's hydroelectric power plant makes electricity. This is used in the homes and industries of Egypt.

▶ The Aswan High Dam is 360 feet high and 2¼ miles long. The hydroelectric power plant makes electricity for industry and also for the many villages along the Nile.

▼ The temples of Abu Simbel stand beside the Nile. They were built over 3,000 years ago by Ramses II, a king of Egypt.

The Ganges

The Ganges River begins on the southern slopes of the Himalayas in India. The river is 1,563 miles long and flows through India into Bangladesh.

The Brahmaputra River rises in the northern Himalayas. The two rivers meet at the Ganges delta in Bangladesh. They fan out into many channels which flow into the Bay of Bengal. The delta is 29,000 square miles in area.

The Holy River

Many people who live by the Ganges believe that the river is holy. They believe that the river can wash away sins. Many people make a special journey to bathe at the holy city of Varanasi. Such a journey is called a **pilgrimage**. There are many religious festivals where pilgrims gather to worship the Ganges. When people die, their bodies are put on wooden rafts. The rafts are set on fire and pushed into the water to float down the river.

A Way of Life

Some 200 million people live along the Ganges. Another 100 million people live in the delta area. The river affects the lives of all these people in one way or another.

Some people farm the fertile flood plain and the delta. Their main crop is rice. Other people make their living by fishing. They hope to catch fish like the katla which can be six feet long and weight 65 pounds.

◀ These people are bathing in the river at the holy city of Varanasi. Varanasi is one of the oldest cities in India. There are 74 special bathing places there.

The area around Patna used to be famous for a cloth colored by a blue **dye** called indigo. Cloth is dyed to color it. People still use water from the Ganges to dye cloth.

The Ganges has been used for trade and travel since early times. The busy port of Calcutta has grown up on the Ganges delta. Nearly half the ships which trade with India come to Calcutta to load and unload their goods.

► These people are dyeing cloth in the Ganges. In India, colors have special meanings. For example, red stands for joy and blue stands for peace.

▼ Many people along the Ganges depend on river fish for food. There are plenty of fish since the waters are clean. Unlike many rivers, the Ganges has not been spoiled by wastes from factories.

The Mississippi

The Mississippi is the longest river in the United States. It rises at Lake Itasca in Minnesota. Hundreds of small rivers join the Mississippi on its 2,375-mile journey south. Its main tributary is the Missouri. Finally, the river winds across a wide flood plain and empties into the Gulf of Mexico.

The Mississippi carries huge amounts of silt along with it. The river drops some of the silt on the river bed. Dredgers clear a way through the muddy, shallow waters. The river pilots have to know exactly where the banks of sand are in order to keep the ships in the deep channels.

The river drops more silt at its mouth where there is a large delta. The delta has grown so much over the years that it now goes a long way out into the Gulf of Mexico. Each year it grows by 330 feet.

▲ The Mississippi has been used for trade for 300 years. Traders found that flat boats were the best type of boat for the shallow river. Steamboats began to replace the flat boats about 175 years ago.

▼ Old sternwheeler steamboats still carry tourists along the Mississippi. The first steamboat sailed on the river in 1811. Twenty years later, more than 1,000 were in use.

From Furs to Oil

The Mississippi was first explored by French people who had settled in Canada. They had come from Canada to look for ways to cross America. A Frenchman called Robert Cavalier traveled down the length of the river to the mouth in 1681. A few years later, the town of New Orleans was founded near the river mouth. The Mississippi was used as a trade route to carry goods. Furs were carried from the north. Tobacco and cotton were grown in the south and taken back to Canada. Boats with flat bottoms were built to use in the shallow river. These flat rafts, or **barges**, floated down the river. A sail was raised for the journey back up the river.

Steamboats began to appear on the river over 150 years ago. These boats were faster than the barges. They soon became a popular way to travel. Today, the steamboats carry tourists.

Oil **refineries** now stand on the banks of the river at Baton Rouge. A refinery is a place where crude oil is made into gasoline

▲ The Mississippi is busy with cargo boats at Baton Rouge, up the river from New Orleans. The string of barges on this side of the river is carrying coal. Oil storage tanks can be seen in the distance.

and other products. Baton Rouge is one of the main oil refineries in the world.

Today, the river is part of the world's largest inland waterway system. Goods can be carried from Tulsa in the west and Pittsburg in the east. A canal links the Mississippi with Chicago.

New Orleans

New Orleans is the second largest port in the United States. Rows of barges carry grain, coal, iron, cotton, tobacco, and oil down the river to the port. There they are loaded on to ships. Goods, like coffee, are brought in to the port from South America.

As a port city, people from many countries have settled there. New Orleans has become a city of music and festivals. It is the home of jazz music. Each year, people pour into New Orleans for the Mardi Gras celebrations.

The Rhine

▼ Three types of transportation can be seen using the Rhine Valley. The barges are slower than the goods train and the trucks, but they are the best way to carry heavy goods.

Like the Mississippi, the Rhine is a very busy river. Millions of tons of cargo travel along the Rhine each year. The Rhine is 1,825 miles long. It rises in Switzerland, crosses western Europe, and empties into the North Sea. The Rhine is linked by canals to other rivers.

A River of Industry

The source of the Rhine is in the Swiss Alps. The river has cut a deep valley through the Alps. It is joined by so many small rivers in the mountains that it becomes wide and strong.

The river then flows into south Germany along a steep valley called the Rhine Gorge. The sides of the hills have been cut by the farmers into wide steps, or **terraces**. Grapes are grown on these terraces. They are used to make wine.

▼ A Rhine barge on the Europa Canal. The canal links the Rhine with the Main River.

In West Germany, the Rhine is joined by another river, the Ruhr. Europe's main coalfield is in this area. Two important industries, steel and coal, have grown up there. The river is used to carry coal, oil, and other heavy goods. It also supplies the water which the many cities and factories along the Rhine need.

The Rhine flows on into the Netherlands where the delta begins. The Netherlands floods easily. Some of the land lies below the level of the sea. The country has a network of canals and ditches to control the floods. The Rhine splits into channels as it makes its way through this land. The main channel is called the Lek River. It flows into the North Sea at Rotterdam. Rotterdam is the world's busiest port. Thousands of barges from the Ruhr area unload their cargoes there. Giant oil tankers bring crude oil to oil refineries near the **docks**.

Boats on the Rhine

There are two main types of shipping on the Rhine. One type is the cruise ship. These ships carry thousands of visitors up the Rhine each year. They stop at old cities like Koblenz, which is at the lower end of the Rhine Gorge.

The other type of shipping is the low, black barge. The Rhine barges are up to 260 feet long and can weigh more than 2,000 tons. The barges pass through the great inland port of Duisburg on their way to ports on the Ruhr, like Essen. People from all over Europe work on the barges. It is a way of life to them. The barge is their work and their home.

▼ Goods from many parts of Europe pass through Rotterdam. The port can handle over 300 oceangoing ships at the same time.

The Murray

The Murray in Australia is 1,625 miles long. It rises in mountains called the Australian Alps. The Murray flows through thick forests to the plains below. The river is joined by several other rivers on its slow journey across the flat plain. These include the Darling and the Murrumbidgee.

A huge irrigation project has made it possible to farm the dry lands along the Murray Valley. Farmers can now grow wheat, rice, fruit, and vines on the irrigated land. Cows and sheep graze on the pastures.

The "Lady Augusta"

People began to settle along the Murray over 100 years ago. Towns and villages grew up, but there were few roads. The best way to carry goods was by river. The **government** of South Australia wanted to make the shipping work faster and better. They offered a large cash prize for the first two steamboats to travel 563 miles up the river. The steamers started at Goolwa, near the river's mouth. They stopped at the place where the Murray met the Darling. The prize was won by Francis Cadell in an iron steamer called the *Lady Augusta*. This was the start of steamboat travel on the Murray.

▲ The Murray is one of the world's great waterways. It meanders past fields of crops and grazing animals for the last 400 miles to the sea.

The *Lady Augusta* won a prize for being the first steamboat to travel up the Murray River to the point where it meets the Darling River.

◄ Dams built for the Snowy Mountains Project made many lakes like this one, Lake Eucumbene. Thousands of workers from all over the world came to work on the Project.

The Snowy Mountain Project

The Snowy Mountains are covered with snow in winter, and they have heavy rainfall in summer. The melting snow and rain fill the Snowy River. This river flows south to the Tasman Sea. Before 1949, most of the water in the river was wasted. It could not be used to irrigate the crops because the river was a long way from the dry plains.

The purpose of the Project was to take water from the Snowy River to the plains. The water is carried through tunnels or channels, called **aqueducts**, to the Murray and Murrumbidgee Rivers. The Project consists of 16 large dams and several smaller ones. There are 80 miles of tunnels through rock, 80 miles of aqueducts, and seven power plants. It took 25 years to finish the work.

The dams across the Snowy River have formed large lakes. The main one is called Lake Eucumbene. The water from these lakes supplies the hydroelectric power plants. They provide enough electicity for two million people.

The Amazon

The Amazon flows through South America for 4,073 miles. Much of the Amazon lies along the **equator**, the imaginary line around the center of the earth. The mouth of the Amazon is 208 miles wide.

The Amazon begins high in the Andes Mountains in Peru. Many other rivers join the Amazon as it flows east through Peru and Brazil. It is so wide and deep that large ships can sail 2,313 miles from the river mouth to Iquitos in Peru. The first 940 miles from the river mouth have an average depth of 293 feet.

▲ An aerial view of the Amazon forest. Palm trees, rubber trees, and Brazil nut trees grow in the thick Amazon rain forest. Some of these trees are 195 feet high.

▼ A riverside market place on the Tapagos River, a tributary of the Amazon. Boats carrying people and goods are starting to arrive.

A Spaniard called Francisco de Orellana made the first journey down the Amazon River in 1541. When he was attacked by local women, he remembered an old story, or **legend**, the Greeks used to tell. It was about fierce women warriors called Amazons. This was how the river got its name.

The Jungle

The Amazon flows through a huge **rain forest**. The weather is always hot, and rain falls almost every day. Plants grow very quickly in this damp, steamy climate. The forest is a tangled mass of tall trees, shrubs, creepers, and twisted tree roots.

People have changed the rivers and the land around them in many parts of the world. The Amazon has been slower to change. Few people live in the forest. The land is not good for farming. Even though some areas have been cleared for timber and minerals, much of the Amazon jungle remains wild. However, it may not stay wild much longer.

There are small villages built of mud and wood on the banks of the river. Some of the huts are raised on poles to avoid flooding. The people fish in the river and farm plots of land on the banks.

Manaus

Manaus is a city in the middle of the jungle. It was built where the Amazon meets another river, the Rio Negro. Manaus was once a very busy port. It was built over 100 years ago so ships could take rubber to the sea. Rubber trees grew wild in the forest around Manaus. Today, most of the world's rubber comes from Southeast Asia, so Manaus is no longer very busy.

▼ The floating dock at Manaus was built for the ships that carried cargoes of rubber along the Amazon. Today, the ships carry other forest products such as nuts, vegetable oils, and wood.

How Lakes are Made

A lake is a large hollow filled with water. The sun makes water evaporate, so a lake always needs a supply of new water. Lakes are filled by rain, streams, and rivers. Sometimes, the lake overflows. Water runs out and starts a new river.

Lakes do not last for ever. Rivers and streams drop silt in the lake. Slowly the hollow is filled in and the lake disappears. Most lakes last for about 100,000 years.

Lakes Made by Glaciers

Lakes can be made in several ways. Many lakes were made during the last **Ice**

► The deep, still waters of a crater lake can look very dark and cold. It is hard to believe that there was once a red-hot volcano here.

Age, which lasted for thousands of years. Great ice sheets covered much of the earth. Heavy glaciers moved slowly across the land. The ice scooped out hollows in the rocky surface. The ice also tore away chunks of rock from the sides of the valleys.

As the glaciers began to melt, they turned into rivers. The rocks were dropped across the valleys. These piles of rocks, or **moraines**, blocked the rivers. The rivers became lakes. Finland, in northern Europe, is dotted with lakes that were made by glaciers.

During the last Ice Age, the ice sheets melted and froze again several times. Rocks were cracked and large pieces were frozen into the ice. The ice and rocks carved out hollows in the land.

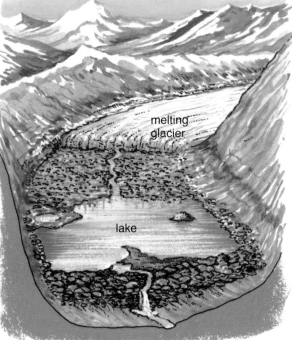

The ice finally melted and dropped the rocks in great piles. Some of the piles of rock blocked the valleys. These valleys filled with water.

Other Kinds of Lakes

Lakes can be made in other ways. A fault in the layers of rock deep in the earth can make parts of the land sink. Then water drains into these areas. Many of the large lakes in Africa were made like this.

Large hollows, called **craters**, are found at the top of old **volcanoes**. These craters can fill with water and turn into lakes. Crater Lake in the United States began in this way. Sometimes the **lava** from a volcano flows across a valley and dams a river. Lake Kivu in Africa was made like this.

Some enormous lakes, or reservoirs, have been made by building dams across rivers. The Bratsk Reservoir in the USSR holds more water than any other lake in the world. There are also large reservoirs in Africa, Europe, and the United States.

▲ The Akosombo Dam in Ghana. Lake Volta, behind the dam, is the largest reservoir in the world in area. The shoreline is 4,531 miles long. The sluice gates near the top of the dam stop the water from overflowing.

The Great Lakes

The Great Lakes lie on the border between the United States and Canada. The five lakes are called Superior, Michigan, Huron, Erie, and Ontario. Lake Superior is the largest freshwater lake in the world. It is 650 feet above sea level. The water is always very cold.

The water from the Great Lakes flows out into the St Lawrence River and links the Great Lakes with the Atlantic Ocean.

▼ Large industrial cities such as Chicago, Detroit, Milwaukee, Cleveland, and Buffalo use the Great Lakes and the St. Lawrence Seaway to transport goods. Eight locks on the Welland Canal take ships 320 feet up or down between Lakes Erie and Ontario.

The St. Lawrence Seaway

The St. Lawrence River flows very fast for 188 miles between Lake Ontario and Montreal in Canada. There are many rapids. There are also rapids between the lakes. This is because they lie at different heights above sea level. The Niagara River plunges over the Niagara Falls between Lakes Erie and Ontario. The United States and Canada decided to build a series of locks and canals so that large ships could travel all the way along the St. Lawrence. They also built dams to provide water for hydroelectric power plants.

The St. Lawrence Seaway was completed in 1959. Most oceangoing ships can now travel from the Atlantic Ocean to Lake Superior. A canal links Chicago, on Lake Michigan, with the Mississippi. During the winter, parts of the Seaway are frozen over. For the rest of the year, goods can be sent by water from Montreal in Canada to New Orleans in the United States.

St Lawrence River

Lake Superior

Montreal

Lake Huron

Lake Ontario

Lake Michigan

ATLANTIC OCEAN

Milwaukee

Detroit

Welland Canal

Chicago

Lake Erie

Cleveland

Lake Erie

sea level

Lake Superior

Lakes Huron and Michigan

Lake Ontario

Using the Waterways

Many different goods come from the area around the Great Lakes. Grain is grown on the land to the west. To the north, the forests of Canada supply trees for timber and papermaking. Iron ore is mined near Lake Superior. There are large coalfields to the south of Lake Erie. All these goods can be carried to the places where they are needed using the waterway system.

The iron ore mined near Lake Superior is taken to the steel mills in Pennsylvania and Ohio. The iron ore is loaded on to a ship at the port on Lake Superior. At the eastern end of Lake Superior, the ship sails along the Soo Canals to avoid the rapids of Sault St. Marie. It crosses Lake Huron and sails through the St. Clair River. Then the ship sails down the Detroit River into Lake Erie. After docking at Cleveland, the iron ore is unloaded and taken to be made into iron and steel.

▲ A cargo ship enters a lock on the St. Lawrence Seaway. The iron bridges at each end have to be raised to allow the ship through.

▼ A tanker on the St. Lawrence River. Ships can sail over 2,190 miles from the Atlantic Ocean to Duluth, on Lake Superior, for most of the year. The Seaway is frozen for about 120 days during the winter.

The African Lakes

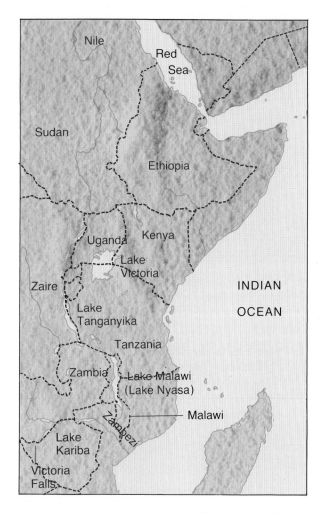

If you look at a map of the eastern side of Africa you will see some large lakes. Among them are Lake Victoria, Lake Tanganyika, and Lake Malawi. Lake Victoria is the second largest freshwater lake in the world. It is 21,828 square miles in area. These lakes also make natural borders between several African countries. Lake Tanganyika separates Zaire from Tanzania.

The lakes were not discovered by Europeans until about 100 years ago. Early explorers sailed around the coast of Africa, but they did not go inland. The first explorer to go into Central Africa was a Scottish doctor called David Livingstone. He found the Victoria Falls and Lake Malawi. He went on to find Lake Tanganyika. This was where he met the American journalist, Henry Stanley, who had been sent to Africa to find Livingstone. Stanley later discovered that Lake Victoria was the source of the White Nile.

▲ The lakes of the eastern side of Africa.

◄ Lake Kariba has become a popular place for tourists. Hotels have been built on the shores of the new lake, and boats carry people to the small islands.

The Rift Valley

When there are two faults in the earth, side by side, the strip of land between them sinks. This becomes a long, broad valley called a **rift valley**.

The Great Rift Valley of Africa is huge. It is 55 miles wide and over 3,125 miles long. It starts at the Red Sea, crosses Ethiopia, and stretches through Uganda, Tanzania, and Malawi. The Rift Valley has two main "arms." **Basins** in the land have filled with water to make lakes. Lake Victoria lies between the two arms. To the west are Lake Tanganyika and Lake Malawi. Other lakes lie to the east of the valley.

Many of the people who live around the lakes are fishermen or farmers. The lakes provide water for rice and other crops.

Reservoirs

Some of the largest dams in the world are in Africa. The reservoirs are huge lakes which provide water for electricity, crops, homes, and industries. Three of the largest reservoirs are Lake Nasser on the Nile, Lake Volta in Ghana, and Lake Kariba on the border between Zambia and Zimbabwe.

Some of the land covered by these lakes was farmed or used by local people. The Batonka people had to move away from the Zambezi Valley when it was flooded and Lake Kariba was made.

▼ A group of fishermen prepare their boats for a day's fishing on Lake Tanganyika. The lake is 425 miles long and in some places is 1,625 feet deep.

Spoiling the Waters

There would be no life on earth without fresh water. Plants could not grow. People and animals could not survive. We have to look after our rivers and lakes, but this does not always happen.

Many of our rivers and lakes have become dirty. Some industries need to use a lot of water. Then, they pump the water back into the rivers. This water is often hot and dirty. Sometimes, the water has chemicals in it. Wildlife and plants are harmed by this water.

The waste water from our homes is called **sewage**. In some countries, raw sewage which has not been treated gets into the rivers. The spoiling of water in this way is called **pollution**.

Life in the Water

There is a natural way of life in unspoiled fresh water. Small fish feed on tiny plants called **plankton**. Large fish eat the small fish. This way of life is upset when the water becomes polluted. The fish and plants need **oxygen** to live. In an unspoiled river, oxygen helps to break down small amounts of waste. If a lot of waste is put into the water, all the oxygen is used up and the fish and plants die.

Other things can also kill the life in the water. Chemicals are put on to the soil to help crops grow. The chemicals flow

◄ The chemicals and waste which pour into a river can kill all the plant and animal life in it. It will be years before the river will be clean again.

slowly through the ground into rivers where they make weeds grow. The water becomes choked, and oxygen is lost. Oil which is spilled from ships lies on the surface of the water. This stops oxygen from getting into the water.

Cleaning the Water

Even fresh water is not pure. It has to be **treated** before it is safe to drink. Drinking untreated water can cause illness. Some countries cannot afford to clean their drinking water. Many people become sick or die because they cannot get clean water to drink. Some people are trying to find new ways of making water clean and safe to drink.

Other countries are trying to stop the pollution of rivers and lakes. They make sure that industries clean their waste water before it is pumped back into the rivers and lakes. Scientists check the water to make sure that it is clean.

We can make our rivers and lakes pure and healthy for all living things. We need to do this so that we can all survive in the future.

▼ Checks are made to see that rivers are not becoming polluted. This scientist is collecting samples of water, animal life, and plant life. The samples will be tested to see if there are any chemicals in them. The amount of oxygen will also be checked.

Glossary

algae: very simple plants. Algae have no leaves, roots, or stems.

aqueduct: a channel made by people for carrying water across a valley or through an underground tunnel.

barge: a wide-bottomed boat. Barges carry goods on rivers and canals.

basin: a wide area of land which makes a large hollow. Some basins fill up with water to make lakes.

canal: a water channel built across the land to join two areas of water. Canals are also built to improve the course of a river and drain the land.

cargo: goods carried by a ship or plane.

chemical: any substance which can change when joined or mixed with another substance.

condensation: the liquid made when a gas changes into a liquid.

condense: to make a gas turn into a liquid.

crater: a deep hollow in a volcano or in the ground, in the shape of a bowl.

dam: a strong wall built to hold back a river. A dam is usually built of concrete, and it is large enough for a lake to be made behind it.

delta: a fan-shaped area of land formed by the mud, sand, and stones dropped by a river at its mouth. The river divides into many channels as it flows through the delta to the sea.

deposit: to leave behind. Rivers deposit sand and stones when they slow down.

dike: a drainage ditch. Also a long, thick, earth wall built to hold back water and control floods.

dock: a place by or on a river, lake, or sea where ships can stop to load and unload.

drain: to pump or channel water away from flooded land. Drained land can be used for farming.

dredger: a machine which brings up mud from the bottom of a river. A dredger works from a boat or from the river bank.

dye: to give new color to something.

electricity: a type of power.

electric shock: a sudden shock made when electrical energy passes through a body.

equator: the imaginary circle around the center of the earth. The hottest parts of the world are nearest to the equator.

erosion: the wearing away of land by water, ice, or the weather. The sea wears away rocks and cliffs. The wind erodes the land by blowing away sand and soil.

estuary: the wide mouth of a river where it meets the sea.

evaporate: to change from a liquid into a gas. Heat from the sun makes water evaporate into the air.

fault: a crack in the rock layers under the surface of the earth. Faults happen when a block of land is pushed up, sinks down, or moves sideways.

ferry: a boat for carrying people and goods across a river.

fertile: describes rich soil where seeds and plants can grow well.

flash flood: a sudden flood caused by very heavy rain.

floodgate: a barrier built across a river to control flooding.

flood plain: the flat area on either side of a river, over which it floods.

fresh water: water that does not contain salt. Fresh water comes from rivers, lakes, and from under the ground.

glacier: a river of slowly moving solid ice.

government: a group of people who control the affairs of the country.

gravity: the force that pulls everything towards the center of the earth. Gravity makes objects fall and gives them weight.

groundwater: the water that is found in the rocks under the surface of the earth.

hydroelectric: describes a way of making electricity by using fast-flowing water to drive a turbine.

Ice Age: a time when much of the world becomes very cold. During the last Ice Age, ice covered large parts of North America and Europe. Ice Ages last for thousands of years. The last one ended 11,000 years ago.

ice cap: a large amount of snow and ice. There is an ice cap around the North Pole and the South Pole.

industry: the work to do with the making or producing of goods.

irrigate: to water the land using a system of pipes and ditches. The water is pumped from rivers, lakes, or from under the ground. Irrigation makes it possible to grow crops in dry places.

lagoon: an area of water which is cut off from the sea by silt.

larva: the second stage in the life of an insect between the egg and the adult.

lava: hot, liquid rock that flows from deep inside the earth. It cools and hardens when it comes to the surface.

legend: an old story, once supposed to be true.

levee: a high earth wall built along the banks of a river to stop flooding. The high banks which develop as a river drops mud are natural levees.

lever: a simple machine for lifting things. It is a stiff, strong bar which can be moved up and down like a seesaw. When one end is moved, the other end moves in the opposite direction and can lift things.

lock: a part of a river or canal with gates at each end. The level of the water can be changed to let ships move "uphill" or "downhill."

mammal: an animal with a warm body which is usually covered with fur. Mammals give birth to live young which feed on the mother's milk.

meander: describes rivers which flow slowly through a valley in large loops or curves.

moraine: the rocks and soil carried along by, or pushed in front of, large sheets of ice. The small hills of rock and soil which are left when the ice melts are also called moraines.

mudflat: a piece of marshy land made by the build-up of mud in wide river mouths.

navigate: to steer or guide a ship.

overshot: turned by water pushing from above.

oxygen: a gas found in the air and in the water which all animals need for breathing.

pilgrimage: a journey to a holy or special place.

pilot: a person who goes on board and steers a ship. A pilot is used when a ship is going in or out of a port, or when it is sailing through dangerous waters.

plankton: tiny plants and animals which float near the surface of inland waters and the seas and oceans.

pollution: the spoiling of air, water, or the land with waste materials, garbage, or fumes.

predator: an animal which lives by hunting and eating other animals.

prey: an animal which is hunted and eaten by other animals for food.

rain forest: a type of forest that grows in the tropics where it is hot and wet.

rapid: a part of the river where the water flows very fast over rocks. The water is usually shallow.

reach: a stage of a river. The stage near the start of a river is called the upper reach.

reed: a water plant with a long strong stalk.

refinery: a place where the raw crude oil from the ground is made pure. Gasoline, diesel oil, and other products are made at refineries.

reptile: a member of a group of animals which have dry, scaly skins and lay eggs with shells. They cannot make their own body heat.

reservoir: a lake which builds up behind a dam.

rift valley: a wide valley which is made by cracks or faults in the earth on each side of the valley.

sewage: the waste matter which is carried away from buildings in pipes.

shaduf: a device for lifting water. A shaduf is made of a pole on a hinge with a bucket at one end and a weight at the other.

shoal: a group of fish.

silt: a mixture of sand and mud carried along and then dropped by a river.

sluice gate: a gate in a waterway which can be either opened to control the amount of water going through or closed to hold the water back.

source: the place where a river begins.

spring: a place where underground water comes to the surface. Springs often trickle out through cracks in the sides of mountains or hills.

steam: the gas which water changes into when it is heated.

swamp: an area of wet, soft land often covered by water.

terrace: a flat piece of ground cut out of a hillside, like a step. Crops can be grown on terraces.

tide: the steady rise and fall of the sea up and down the shore. There are two high tides and two low tides about every 24 hours.

trade: to do business by buying and selling goods.

treat: to break down poisons in waste material by adding something, usually chemicals, to it.

tributary: a stream or river which flows into a large river.

tropical: describes something to do with, or coming from, the tropics. The tropics are the hot parts of the world near the equator.

turbine: a wheel with many curved blades. It is turned by water or a gas. Turbines drive the machines which make electricity.

undershot: turned by water pushing from below.

valley: low-lying land between hills.

vapor: a gas or cloud of tiny droplets of a substance, such as steam.

volcano: a type of mountain through which hot, liquid rock comes out from deep inside the earth.

water cycle: describes the movement of water from the air to the ground and sea and back again to the air.

webbed feet: describes the type of feet which some water animals have. Webbed feet have toes joined by a layer of skin. This helps the animal paddle through the water.

Index